NAUGHTY
OR
NICE?

The Ultimate Collection of Sexy Games for Couples

Would You Rather...?
Truth or Dare?
Never Have I Ever...

J.R. James

Table of Contents

Spice up your love life even more, and explore all the discussion books for couples by J.R. James:

Love and Relationship Books for Couples

Would You Rather...? The Romantic Conversation Game for Couples (Love and Romance Edition)

Sexy Game Books for Couples

Would You Rather...? The Naughty Conversation Game for Couples (Hot and Sexy Edition)

Truth or Dare? The Sexy Game of Naughty Choices (Hot and Wild Edition)

Never Have I Ever... An Exciting and Sexy Game for Adults (Hot and Dirty Edition)

The Hot or Not Quiz for Couples: The Sexy Game of Naughty Questions and Revealing Answers

Pillow Talk: The Sexy Game of Naughty Trivia Questions for Couples

The Naughty Newlywed Game: A Sexy Game of Questions for Couples

Sexy Discussion Books for Couples

Let's Talk Sexy: Essential Conversation Starters to Explore Your Lover's Secret Desires and Transform Your Sex Life

All **THREE** *Let's Talk About...* sexy question books in one massive volume for one low price. Save now!

Let's Talk About... Sexual Fantasies and Desires: Questions and Conversation Starters for Couples Exploring Their Sexual Interests

Let's Talk About... Non-Monogamy: Questions and Conversation Starters for Couples Exploring Open Relationships, Swinging, or Polyamory

Let's Talk About... Kinks and Fetishes: Questions and Conversation Starters for Couples Exploring Their Sexual Wild Side

Change your sex life forever through the power of sexy fun with your spouse, partner, or lover!

www.sexygamesforcouples.com

Sexy Vacations for Couples
https://geni.us/Passion

WOULD YOU RATHER...?

The Naughty Conversation Game for Couples

HOT AND SEXY EDITION

J.R. James

HOW TO PLAY THE GAME

The rules for this game are very simple:

There needs to be at least two people to play. (It's a great game for couples!) If you and your partner are really adventurous, try playing with another couple, or even more people at a party. The more people, the more fun!

Each page has a hypothetical question that begins with "Would you rather...?" and ends with two choices. Take turns asking and answering the questions. **You must choose one of the options, and no skipping the questions.**

As you spend time discussing the answers, you'll soon you'll find yourselves smiling, laughing, and enjoying the sexually charged conversation. Who knows? You may even discover new sexual possibilities for your relationship. Just have fun! It's the game where everyone wins!

Enjoy!

1
Would you rather...

Watch your partner have a hot and heavy make out session with someone you don't know,

OR

Listen to them have loud, wild sex behind closed doors with someone you do know?

2

Would you rather...

Never have another orgasm for the rest of your life,

OR

Have a perpetual orgasm that never stops?

<u>3</u>

Would you rather…

Try something new and kinky in bed,

OR

Have "typical", but very passionate sex?

<u>4</u>

Would you rather…

Have orgasms that last three times longer than normal,

OR

Have sex three times more often than you typically do?

5
Would you rather…

Go to work or school completely naked for one day,

OR

Be naked every time you're in the car for the next year?

<u>6</u>

Would you rather...

Be a terrible kisser,

OR

Be awful at oral sex?

7
Would you rather…

Accidentally send nude photos to your ex,

OR

Accidentally send them to a neighbor?

_8_

Would you rather...

Have public sex in a nearly empty sports stadium during a game,

OR

Have sex in a darkened, but crowded, movie theater?

<u>9</u>

Would you rather…

Have your lover kiss every square inch of your body,

OR

Have your lover lick you from head to toe?

10

Would you rather…

Be able to make yourself orgasm any time you like,

OR

Be able to make anyone else orgasm at will?

_11_

Would you rather...

Have sex with a biter,

OR

Have sex with a screamer?

12

Would you rather...

Be a porn star,

OR

Date a porn star?

13
Would you rather…

Make out with a person wearing clown makeup,

OR

A person who is dressed in a realistic zombie costume?

14

Would you rather…

Be really good at foreplay and bad at sex,

OR

Be really good at sex and terrible at foreplay?

_15_

Would you rather…

Have sex with only one person all your life,

OR

Always have sex in the same position?

_16_

Would you rather…

Wear nipple clamps for an entire day,

OR

Have a small dildo in your ass for the day?

17
Would you rather…

Have a lover who never stops talking during sex,

OR

Have one that never makes a sound?

_18_

Would you rather…

Watch your ex having sex,

OR

Have your ex watch you having sex?

19

Would you rather...

Masturbate in front of a crowd,

OR

Watch a crowd of people masturbate in front of you?

_20_

Would you rather…

Use chocolate syrup during sex,

OR

Use whipped cream?

21

Would you rather...

Have a lover who is slow, gentle, and can last for hours,

OR

Have a lover who's passionate and energetic, but can only last a few minutes?

22

Would you rather...

Cry every time you orgasmed,

OR

Laugh uncontrollably?

23
Would you rather…

Have sex outside in the middle of a hurricane,

OR

In a blizzard?

24

Would you rather...

Take a lover with terrible body odor,

OR

One with horribly bad breath?

25

Would you rather...

Have a partner who can never lie (even if the truth is painful to hear),

OR

Be with a partner who always says what you want to hear (even if it's not true)?

_26_

Would you rather…

Give a golden shower,

OR

Receive one?

<u>27</u>
Would you rather…

Have a lover who can never orgasm,

OR

One that can never make you orgasm?

<u>28</u>

Would you rather...

Date someone with a perfect body, but who's boring in bed,

OR

Date someone who's amazing in bed, but who looks average?

29

Would you rather…

Give up masturbating for a year,

OR

Give up sex for 4 months?

30

Would you rather…

Be with a lover who has no hair anywhere on their head or body,

OR

Have one who is excessively hairy everywhere?

_31_

Would you rather...

Your partner found oral sex disgusting,

OR

Was constantly obsessed with anal sex?

32

Would you rather...

Sleep with the movie or music star of your choice,

OR

Have sex with any sports star or athlete?

33

Would you rather...

Be with a lover who would try anything you could ever want in bed, but is bad at sex,

OR

Have a lover who is great at sex, but extremely limited in what they would do?

_34_

Would you rather…

Have sex with your partner all day long,

OR

Have sex with your partner all night long?

_35_

Would you rather…

Give a handjob to your partner in public,

OR

Receive a handjob from your lover in public?

36

Would you rather…

Work at a strip club,

OR

Have a partner who works
at a strip club?

37

Would you rather…

Always have sex before breakfast,

OR

Only have sex after dinner?

38

Would you rather…

Accidentally scream the wrong name in bed,

OR

Hear your partner scream the wrong name in bed?

39

Would you rather…

Have your toes sucked
during sex,

OR

Have your fingers sucked
during sex?

<u>40</u>

Would you rather…

Be with a lover who was incredibly romantic,

OR

Have a lover who was super kinky?

41

Would you rather...

Be told you were terrible at kissing,

OR

Be told you were awful at oral sex?

42

Would you rather…

Have sex in bright lighting,

OR

Have sex in complete
darkness?

43

Would you rather…

Loudly announce your dirtiest sexual fantasies in front of your co-workers,

OR

In front of your family reunion?

_44_

Would you rather…

Laugh uncontrollably during sex,

OR

Cry inconsolably during foreplay?

45

Would you rather…

Watch something erotic with your lover,

OR

Listen to your lover read erotica while you touch yourself?

<u>46</u>
Would you rather...

Have a threesome,

OR

Participate in an orgy?

47

Would you rather...

Pay for sex,

OR

Get paid for it?

<u>48</u>

Would you rather…

Watch a girl on girl video,

OR

Watch a guy on guy?

<u>49</u>

Would you rather...

Only be able to have sex in cars,

OR

Only be able to have sex in the shower?

50

Would you rather…

Never be able to masturbate again,

OR

Never be able to eat solid foods again?

51

Would you rather...

Have an obvious orgasm every time you or someone else says your name,

OR

Orgasm every time you're near a piece of fruit?

52
Would you rather...

Feel horny all the time, but never have sex,

OR

Never feel aroused, but be able to have sex whenever you'd like?

53

Would you rather…

Date someone much, much more attractive than you,

OR

Date someone slightly less attractive?

54

Would you rather…

Your partner insist on wearing an animal costume during sex,

OR

Have them insist on you wearing the costume?

55

Would you rather…

Go out for a wild night on the town,

OR

Have a cozy, intimate evening at home?

56

Would you rather…

Be with a partner who was excessively affectionate in public,

OR

Who never showed affection in public?

57

Would you rather…

Fall asleep with your lover,

OR

Wake up next to them?

58

Would you rather…

Have sex on live television,

OR

Never have sex ever again?

_59_

Would you rather…

Have your lover be more dominant in bed,

OR

Have your lover be more submissive?

_60_

Would you rather…

Watch a porno starring all of your co-workers,

OR

Or all of your partner's exes?

61

Would you rather…

Watch your partner masturbate,

OR

Have your partner watch you masturbate?

62

Would you rather…

Find out your partner is secretly a stripper,

OR

Find out they're a high-priced prostitute?

63

Would you rather…

Have more foreplay in
your life,

OR

Have more sex?

<u>64</u>

Would you rather…

Give up kissing for the rest of your life,

OR

Give up any foreplay?

65

Would you rather...

Be with a lover who's abnormally tall,

OR

Incredibly short?

66

Would you rather...

Only be able to have sex at work for the rest of your life,

OR

Or only ever be able to have sex outside?

<u>67</u>

Would you rather…

Have your partner fall asleep every time the two of you are having sex ,

OR

Will only agree to sex between the hours of 9 a.m. to 3 p.m.?

_68_

Would you rather...

Talk dirty to your lover while they're trying to work,

OR

Listen to them talk dirty to you while you're trying to work?

69

Would you rather…

Have sex in a hot tub with another couple,

OR

Have sex in a pool with lots of people around?

_70_

Would you rather…

Go to work with your neck covered in hickeys,

OR

Go to a family celebration covered in them?

TRUTH OR DARE?

The Sexy Game of Naughty Choices

HOT AND WILD EDITION

HOW TO PLAY THE GAME

The rules for this game are very simple:

There needs to be at least two people to play. (It's the perfect game for couples!) The Dares are worded in such a manner that you can either play an intimate game with your significant other, or you can play with a group of people. So, if you and your partner are really adventurous, try playing with another couple or even more people at a party. The more people, the more fun!

Each page consists of a Truth (question) and a Dare (something the player must do). Take turns asking one another to choose either a Truth or a Dare. If you are the one asking, do not reveal the question or the dare, your partner must make the choice blindly. If your partner chooses "Truth", you'll ask the question(s) on the page and they must honestly answer. If they choose "Dare", they must do exactly what the dare instructs them to do. **Your partner cannot know what the truth or dare is ahead of time, and no skipping pages. (NOTE: If playing in a group, you cannot choose the same person twice in a row to help you complete a Dare. You must alternate partners.)** <u>Consent is key, so please have the consent of all players involved before any dare is played. And as always, please practice safe sex.</u>

No matter which choice you make, the game will lead you into hot conversations and sexy physical scenarios. Who knows? You may even discover new sexual possibilities for your relationships. Just have fun! It's the game where everyone wins!

1
Truth or Dare?

TRUTH: Have you ever had a threesome? If not, would you consider it? Who would you choose as your third?

OR

DARE: Fake an orgasm while looking into someone's eyes.

2
Truth or Dare?

TRUTH: Who are three people you would love to sleep with if you had the chance?

OR

DARE: For 30 seconds, whisper sexy, dirty things you'd like to do in someone's ear.

3
Truth or Dare?

TRUTH: Have you ever had sex with someone without knowing their name? If not, would you have to know someone's name in order to have sex with them?

OR

DARE: Slowly tease someone with your tongue anywhere on their head, neck, or face.

4
Truth or Dare?

TRUTH: Have you ever watched someone else have sex? If not, name one couple who you'd like to watch.

OR

DARE: Demonstrate your most flexible sex move.

5

Truth or Dare?

TRUTH: What's the last sexual dream you had and who was in it?

OR

DARE: Take off your shirt and dance in front of an open window or door for 1 minute.

6
Truth or Dare?

TRUTH: What's something most people don't like in bed, but you can't get enough of?

OR

DARE: Using your phone or computer, search for a difficult sexual position from the Kama Sutra and try it out with a partner for 3 minutes.

7
Truth or Dare?

TRUTH: Have you ever sent or received nude photos? If not, pick one person whom you'd send them to if you had to.

OR

DARE: Take a very sexy photo of yourself on someone else's cellphone.

8
Truth or Dare?

TRUTH: Have you ever had sex in a public place? If not, where would you consider doing it?

OR

DARE: Take off someone's shirt using only your lips and teeth.

<u>9</u>
Truth or Dare?

TRUTH: Who's the most "inappropriate" person you've ever had a fantasy about?

OR

DARE: Pick a player and using your mouth, make your way from their wrist to their ear. Make it slow and seductive!

10
Truth or Dare?

TRUTH: Have you ever had a sexual experience at work?

OR

DARE: Using only your fingertips, try to give another player goosebumps.

11
Truth or Dare?

TRUTH: What's a secret fantasy of yours that you've never shared with anyone else?

OR

DARE: Make out with someone for 30 seconds with your eyes covered.

12
Truth or Dare?

TRUTH: Have you ever been in a sex video?

OR

DARE: Have someone record you on video doing something sexy.

_13_
Truth or Dare?

TRUTH: What's the dirtiest text message you've ever sent?

OR

DARE: Send a dirty text message to someone in the room.

14

Truth or Dare?

TRUTH: What was the worst sexual experience you've ever had?

OR

DARE: For 1 minute, demonstrate your idea of amazing foreplay with someone.

15
Truth or Dare?

TRUTH: How many sexual partners have you had in your life? Would you like that number to be higher or lower?

OR

DARE: Choose a partner and starting at their navel, softly kiss your way up their chest and neck, up to their lips.

16
Truth or Dare?

TRUTH: What's your favorite sex toy? If you don't have one, which one would you like to try?

OR

DARE: Gently tease someone's ear using only the tip of your tongue.

17
Truth or Dare?

TRUTH: Would you star in a professional porno for $5000? How about $500? $50?

OR

DARE: Use your tongue to spell out something sexy on someone's body.

18
Truth or Dare?

TRUTH: Have another player ask you any question they desire!

OR

DARE: Give an erotic striptease and remove at least three items of clothing.

19

Truth or Dare?

TRUTH: If you and your partner had to swap with another couple, which couple would you choose?

OR

DARE: Pick a spot on someone's body that isn't usually considered sexual and seductively shower it with kisses.

20

Truth or Dare?

TRUTH: What's your favorite sexual position and why?

OR

DARE: Try and turn someone on using touch, but you can only touch their arms and hands.

<u>21</u>
Truth or Dare?

TRUTH: What's one kink or fetish you've always been curious to try?

OR

DARE: Swap underwear or other piece of clothing with another player and wear it for 2 rounds.

<u>22</u>
Truth or Dare?

TRUTH: What's the most embarrassing sexual experience of your life?

OR

DARE: Sensually massage someone's pubic area, through their clothing, for 30 seconds.

23
Truth or Dare?

TRUTH: What are three "non-sexual" things that turn you on?

OR

DARE: Eat a piece of food as erotically as you can.

24

Truth or Dare?

TRUTH: How would you rate your skills in the bedroom and explain why?

OR

DARE: Pick someone and as seductively as you can, demonstrate how you would hit on them in a bar.

25
Truth or Dare?

TRUTH: Have you ever hit on someone else's significant other, or had them hit on you?

OR

DARE: Have the last person who completed a dare, give you a dare of their choice.

26

Truth or Dare?

TRUTH: Have you ever given or received a "golden shower?" If not, are you interested?

OR

DARE: Show the other player(s) all the areas you like to be teased or touched. Demonstrate how you like to be touched.

27

Truth or Dare?

TRUTH: Excluding your current significant other, who in your past was amazing in bed?

OR

DARE: Using your sexiest voice, tell someone three things you find attractive about them.

<u>28</u>
Truth or Dare?

TRUTH: Have you ever had a same-sex experience? (Alternate: Have you ever had an opposite-sex experience?)

OR

DARE: Lie down, have someone blindfold you, and let them use their fingertips or something soft to lightly trace your body's curves for 1 minute.

29

Truth or Dare?

TRUTH: What was your first sexual experience and would you have changed anything about it?

OR

DARE: Kiss and lick someone's lips and try to get them to lose control and kiss you back.

30
Truth or Dare?

TRUTH: If you could only have anal sex or oral sex for the rest of your life, which would you choose?

OR

DARE: Pick a partner and blindfold yourself. You have to give a passionate kiss to whatever part of their body they put in front of your mouth.

31
Truth or Dare?

TRUTH: How many times a week do you masturbate? Where do you normally do it?

OR

DARE: Pretend you're a porn star and describe in detail what and who you would do in your first porn video.

32

Truth or Dare?

TRUTH: Have you ever gone skinny dipping or streaking? If not, would you?

OR

DARE: Play a sexy song, and pick a partner to dirty dance with for the length of the song.

33

Truth or Dare?

TRUTH: Have you ever had any sexual fantasies about a fictional character?

OR

DARE: Pick someone, turn off the lights, and tease them any way you like for 1 minute.

34

Truth or Dare?

TRUTH: What's one fantasy you've had that you've never shared with anyone else?

OR

DARE: Slowly and seductively, suck on someone's fingers.

35
Truth or Dare?

TRUTH: What do you think are your most attractive physical qualities?

OR

DARE: Play the next round only in your underwear.

36
Truth or Dare?

TRUTH: If you were to throw an orgy, who are six people you'd invite to it?

OR

DARE: With a partner, act out an intro for a cheesy porn movie.

37

Truth or Dare?

TRUTH: What was the first dirty movie/porno you watched?

OR

DARE: Choose a food item such as chocolate sauce or whipped cream and lick it off of someone's body. (But not on the penis or vagina… yet.)

_38_

Truth or Dare?

TRUTH: If you were to be a stripper, what are five songs you'd dance to?

OR

DARE: Charades! Silently act out a sexual act or term and have the other player(s) guess what it is. The winner gets a hot kiss.

39
Truth or Dare?

TRUTH: What's one thing you'd like to do better in bed?

OR

DARE: Ask for a volunteer, then using a ruler or similar object, give them a spanking.

_40_

Truth or Dare?

TRUTH: What's one of the kinkiest things you've ever done?

OR

DARE: Slide your hand down your pants (or up your dress) and pleasure yourself for 1 minute.

41

Truth or Dare?

TRUTH: Can you recall one orgasm or sexual experience that stands above all others?

OR

DARE: Give someone in the room a sensual butt massage for 1 minute.

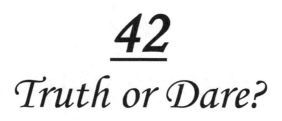 42
Truth or Dare?

TRUTH: Have another player ask you any question they desire!

OR

DARE: Masturbate while you pleasure another player only using your feet. Do this for 2 minutes.

43
Truth or Dare?

TRUTH: How many times a week do you typically have an orgasm?

OR

DARE: Pick someone in the room and for 30 seconds beg them to have sex with you. List all the ways you'd pleasure them in bed.

44

Truth or Dare?

TRUTH: What's the most erotic thing you've ever read?

OR

DARE: Choose a partner, and then flip a coin. If the coin comes up "Heads", then you have to do anything your partner says to do for 30 seconds. If it lands on "Tails", then flash everyone in the room.

45

Truth or Dare?

TRUTH: What do you think are the best techniques for great oral sex?

OR

DARE: Have someone in the room do a body shot off of you with the drink of their choice.

46

Truth or Dare?

TRUTH: How much money would it take for you to have sex with an attractive stranger? An average stranger?

OR

DARE: Ask for a volunteer, then take a small piece of candy or food and put in your mouth. Without using your hands, transfer the candy from your mouth to theirs.

47

Truth or Dare?

TRUTH: What's the longest sexual experience you've ever had? How long was it?

OR

DARE: Give someone a foot massage for 1 minute while telling a dirty story.

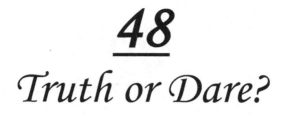

48
Truth or Dare?

TRUTH: If you had to choose between rough and passionate sex or slow and gentle love-making for the rest of your life, which would you choose?

OR

DARE: On a computer or phone, find a porn video to show the other players. Explain what it is you like about this particular video.

49
Truth or Dare?

TRUTH: Have you ever had sex in a car, boat, or plane? If so, explain the experience.

OR

DARE: Have the other players pick out a sexy outfit or piece of clothing for you to wear for three rounds.

50

Truth or Dare?

TRUTH: What's one thing you'd like your sexual partner(s) to do better in bed?

OR

DARE: Have someone draw a "tattoo" on you in a location that's normally covered by clothing. Have them draw either a dirty picture or phrase.

51
Truth or Dare?

TRUTH: How many one night stands have you had?

OR

DARE: Using only your feet, try for 1 minute to get someone physically aroused.

52

Truth or Dare?

TRUTH: Have you ever paid for sex? If not, would you consider paying for it if the person was a hot celebrity?

OR

DARE: Have the last person who completed a dare, give you a dare of their choice.

53
Truth or Dare?

TRUTH: What is your idea of perfect foreplay?

OR

DARE: Twerk in only your underwear.

_54_

Truth or Dare?

TRUTH: What role-playing fantasy would you like to try?

OR

DARE: Suck, lick, and kiss a partner's belly button and waistline for 1 minute.

55
Truth or Dare?

TRUTH: What is the one part of your body you consider your "sweet spot"?

OR

DARE: Ask for a volunteer, then put your hand down their underwear and keep it there for 1 round.

56
Truth or Dare?

TRUTH: Do you prefer spitting or swallowing?

OR

DARE: Blindfold yourself, then for 30 seconds let the other player(s) silently try and turn you on.

57

Truth or Dare?

TRUTH: If you could make three people orgasm right now, who would you choose?

OR

DARE: Have the other player(s) completely undress you. Stay naked for 2 rounds.

58

Truth or Dare?

TRUTH: What is your least favorite sexual position and why?

OR

DARE: Give a player a long, wet kiss on the ass.

<u>59</u>
Truth or Dare?

TRUTH: What was one lie you've told someone concerning sex?

OR

DARE: Tell a dirty story for 2 minutes, and use as many nasty words and sexual terms as you can.

<u>60</u>

Truth or Dare?

TRUTH: What's your dirtiest secret wish?

OR

DARE: Go into a separate room and call one of the other players. Give them hot phone sex for 2 minutes.

61
Truth or Dare?

TRUTH: What do you fantasize or think about when you masturbate?

OR

DARE: Face a partner and straddle them for the next 2 rounds. Gently grind on them while the game continues.

<u>62</u>

Truth or Dare?

TRUTH: Do you have any sexual regrets? If so, what are they?

OR

DARE: Pick any book or magazine and read it out loud as seductively as possible.

63

Truth or Dare?

TRUTH: Do you prefer domination or submission in bed?

OR

DARE: Gently kiss and lick the inside of another player's bare thighs for 1 minute.

<u>64</u>

Truth or Dare?

TRUTH: Have you ever been to a sex club? If not, would you be willing to go?

OR

DARE: Leave a hickey on a player in a place normally covered by clothing.

<u>65</u>

Truth or Dare?

TRUTH: Has anyone ever caught you having sex? If so, describe what happened.

OR

DARE: Pick a partner and pleasure them with your hand as they pleasure you with theirs. Enjoy each other in this way for 2 minutes.

66

Truth or Dare?

TRUTH: Have you ever orgasmed while fully clothed? If so, explain what happened.

OR

DARE: For 30 seconds, remove your shirt and pinch your nipples in front of the other players. Moan while you're doing it.

67
Truth or Dare?

TRUTH: Have you ever fantasized about watching your significant other with someone else?

OR

DARE: Using someone else's fingers, show them how and where you like to be touched.

68

Truth or Dare?

TRUTH: What is one thing you'd never do in bed no matter what?

OR

DARE: Have the last person who completed a dare, give you a dare of their choice.

69

Truth or Dare?

TRUTH: Have you ever left or kicked someone out immediately after having sex?

OR

DARE: Choose a partner and get into the "69" position. The two of you can kiss, lick, or tease anywhere on the thighs for 1 minute. No straying to the sweet spot!

70

Truth or Dare?

TRUTH: What was your first experience with masturbation like?

OR

DARE: In any way you can, try and make another player orgasm in 4 minutes or less. The only condition is they must stay clothed.

NEVER HAVE I EVER...

An Exciting and Sexy Game for Adults

HOT AND DIRTY EDITION

HOW TO PLAY THE GAME

The rules for this game are very simple, if a little different than the typical *Never Have I Ever..* game:

There needs to be at least two people to play. (It's a great game for new couples to learn about each other!) If you and your partner are really adventurous, try playing with another couple, or even more people at a party. The more people, the more fun!

Each page has a statement that begins with "Never have I ever...". One player should read the statement in its entirety. Each player will then consider if the statement is true for them, and if it is, they will hold up a finger. For example: Seth and Lucy are playing together. Seth reads, "Never have I ever... Had a threesome." Seth has never had a ménage a trois, so he doesn't do anything. Lucy has had a threesome, so she holds up one finger. (You can use anything to keep score, not just fingers.) After ten statements, there is a prize page. **Whoever has the highest score with the most fingers up is the winner of the round and wins the prize.** It's a game that rewards a player's naughty, sexy past! The player with the lowest score needs to follow the directions on the prize page to reward the winner. If there are more than two people playing, then the winner is the person with the highest score, and the loser is the one with the lowest score. After the prize is completed, reset the scores and start a new round.

As you spend time discussing the answers, you'll soon you'll find yourselves smiling, laughing, and enjoying the sexually charged conversation. Who knows? You may even discover new sexual possibilities for your relationship. Just have fun, because it's the game where everyone wins!

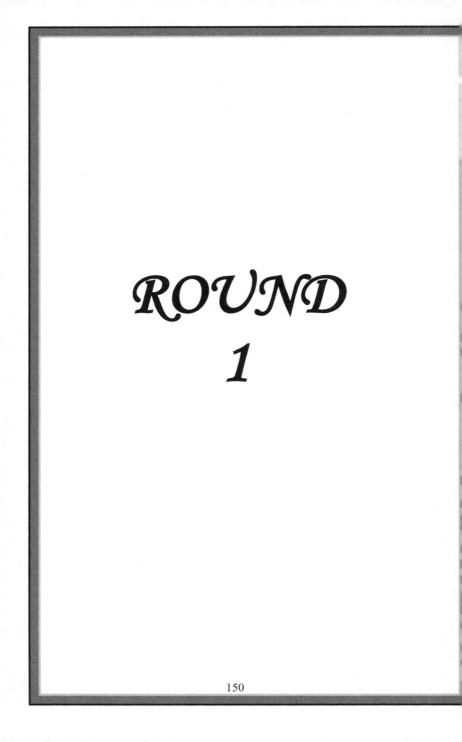

ROUND

1

1

Never have I ever…

Had sex while at school or work.

2

Never have I ever…

Accidentally sent nudes or naughty texts to the wrong person.

3

Never have I ever…

Masturbated in front of someone else.

4

Never have I ever…

Watched another couple having sex.

5

Never have I ever...

Had a fantasy involving
one of my teachers.

6

Never have I ever...

Made a sex video.

7

Never have I ever…

Used food during sex.

8

Never have I ever…

Had sex in a public area.

9

Never have I ever...

Slept with someone without knowing their first name.

10

Never have I ever...

Given or received a golden shower.

Prize Page

The winner of this round gets to choose what the loser has to wear, or not wear, for the next three rounds.

ROUND
2

11

Never have I ever…

Had sex with a screamer or a biter.

12

Never have I ever…

Faked an orgasm.

_13_

Never have I ever…

Lied to someone about how good they were in bed.

_14_

Never have I ever…

Left work early to have sex.

15

Never have I ever…

Given a sexy striptease set to music.

16

Never have I ever…

Mistakenly called someone the wrong name in bed.

17

Never have I ever...

Sucked someone's toes or had my toes sucked.

18

Never have I ever...

Flirted with someone when I knew they were taken.

<u>19</u>

Never have I ever...

Watched somebody else masturbate.

<u>20</u>

Never have I ever...

Had sex with someone with terrible body odor.

Prize Page

The loser has to try and make the winner moan in pleasure within two minutes. You can do it in whatever way you think will work the quickest.

ROUND
3

21

Never have I ever…

Gone more than a year
between sexual encounters.

22

Never have I ever…

Had anal sex.

23

Never have I ever…

Fooled around with
someone famous.

24

Never have I ever…

Given or received a
handjob in a public place.

25

Never have I ever...

Given or received a lap dance.

26

Never have I ever...

Had a one night stand.

27

Never have I ever...

Had a threesome.

28

Never have I ever...

Watched a porn video
together with a lover.

29

Never have I ever...

Had a sexual experience with someone of the same sex. (Alternate: With someone of the opposite sex.)

30

Never have I ever...

Swapped partners with another couple.

Prize Page

The loser of this round has to send a very sexy selfie with a dirty text to the winner's phone.

ROUND
4

31

Never have I ever…

Had sex while I was tied up.

32

Never have I ever…

Joined the mile high club. (Had a sexual experience on a plane.)

33

Never have I ever...

Been to a nude beach or
resort.

34

Never have I ever...

Had a sexual fling with
someone ten years older or
younger than myself.

35

Never have I ever...

Been handcuffed to a bed.

36

Never have I ever...

Had a sexual fantasy about
a co-worker.

37

Never have I ever...

Had sex in a pool or hot tub.

38

Never have I ever...

Had an "innocent" massage lead to sex.

39

Never have I ever...

Had pity sex with someone.

40

Never have I ever...

Had a crush on a friend's parent.

Prize Page

The loser of this round needs to softly tease the winner's chest, neck, and ears with their lips and tongue for one minute.

ROUND
5

41

Never have I ever...

Had sex while I was really drunk.

42

Never have I ever...

Had sex in a quiet public location, such as a library or a museum.

<u>43</u>

Never have I ever...

Played the role as a lover's sex slave.

<u>44</u>

Never have I ever...

Licked someone's anus, or had mine licked.

45

Never have I ever…

Read an erotic novel.

46

Never have I ever…

Kicked someone out right after sex.

47

Never have I ever…
Fallen asleep during sex.

48

Never have I ever…
Slept with a stripper.

<u>49</u>

Never have I ever…

Had sex in the woods.

<u>50</u>

Never have I ever…

Eavesdropped on someone else having sex.

Prize Page

The winner of this round gets to pick any part of their body and have the loser sensually and seductively kiss it for two minutes.

ROUND
6

51

Never have I ever…

Been spanked with a belt,
whip, or paddle.

52

Never have I ever…

Had a sexual encounter in
a public restroom.

53

Never have I ever...
Done a body shot.

54

Never have I ever...
Had a sexual fantasy come true.

55

Never have I ever…

Bought a sex toy.

56

Never have I ever…

Had a sexual experience in
a darkened movie theater.

57

Never have I ever...

Licked chocolate syrup or
whipped cream off of
someone.

58

Never have I ever...

Watched a significant other
have sex with someone
else.

59

Never have I ever...

Tried a sexual position
from the Kama Sutra.

60

Never have I ever...

Played strip poker.

Prize Page

The winner of this round gets to choose a food item, place it anywhere on their body, and have the loser lick it off of them. (The winner can switch roles if they so choose, and lick it off of the loser instead.)

ROUND
7

61

Never have I ever...

Been to a sex club.

62

Never have I ever...

Had sex while blindfolded.

_63_

Never have I ever…

Flirted with someone else
in front of a significant
other.

_64_

Never have I ever…

Had sex without any
kissing involved.

65

Never have I ever...

Tried Tantric sex.

66

Never have I ever...

Been to any sort of sex class.

67
Never have I ever...
Had someone take sexy
photos of me.

68
Never have I ever...
Had sex more than four
times in a day.

69

Never have I ever…

Shaved someone else's
pubic area.

70

Never have I ever…

Given a partner a "hall
pass" (temporary
permission to sleep with
someone else).

Prize Page

The loser has to give the winner a foot massage for two minutes while telling the them all the ways they are amazing in bed. (If you don't know how they are in bed, then make it up.)

ROUND
8

71

Never have I ever…
Had sex on a beach.

72

Never have I ever…
Used a sex swing.

73

Never have I ever...

Teased a lover with ice cubes.

74

Never have I ever...

Tried any kind of BDSM during sex.

75

Never have I ever…

Visited a strip club.

76

Never have I ever…

Had sex in front of an open window.

77

Never have I ever…

Had sex with more than
five people in a year.

78

Never have I ever…

Been walked in on while
having sex.

79

Never have I ever...

Used an internet video
camera to have "sex."

80

Never have I ever...

Made someone orgasm in
under a minute.

Prize Page

The loser has to gently tease and pleasure the winner using only their hands and fingertips for three minutes.

ROUND
9

81

Never have I ever…

Made out with two people
at the same time.

82

Never have I ever…

Been gagged during sex.

83

Never have I ever…

Had sex with a virgin.

84

Never have I ever…

Had a sexual fantasy about
an animated character.

_85_

Never have I ever…

Had my nipples or genitals pierced.

_86_

Never have I ever…

Been injured during sex.

87

Never have I ever…

Gone more than a month without masturbating.

88

Never have I ever…

Slept in the nude all night.

89

Never have I ever…
Talked dirty to a lover
during sex.

90

Never have I ever…
Roleplay while in costume.

Prize Page

The loser has to orally pleasure the winner for two minutes in whatever way they wish.

ROUND 10

91

Never have I ever…

Worn a chastity device.

92

Never have I ever…

Participated in an orgy.

93

Never have I ever...

Had sex on a boat.

94

Never have I ever...

Made out with a complete
stranger.

<u>95</u>

Never have I ever…

Been caught masturbating.

<u>96</u>

Never have I ever…

Flirted with a teacher or a boss.

97

Never have I ever…

Made a purchase at an
Adult store.

98

Never have I ever…

Made someone orgasm
while they were fully
clothed.

99

Never have I ever…
Worn a very sexy
Halloween costume.

100

Never have I ever…
Flashed someone.

Reverse Prize Page

Including this round, identify which player has lost the most rounds during the entire game.

This deprived individual needs some extra sexy experiences. For this last round, the most winning player of the game has to make one sexual fantasy come true for the player who lost the most rounds

Spice up your love life even more, and explore all the discussion books for couples by J.R. James:

Love and Relationship Books for Couples

Would You Rather...? The Romantic Conversation Game for Couples (Love and Romance Edition)

Sexy Game Books for Couples

Would You Rather...? The Naughty Conversation Game for Couples (Hot and Sexy Edition)

Truth or Dare? The Sexy Game of Naughty Choices (Hot and Wild Edition)

Never Have I Ever... An Exciting and Sexy Game for Adults (Hot and Dirty Edition)

The Hot or Not Quiz for Couples: The Sexy Game of Naughty Questions and Revealing Answers

Pillow Talk: The Sexy Game of Naughty Trivia Questions for Couples

The Naughty Newlywed Game: A Sexy Game of Questions for Couples

Sexy Discussion Books for Couples

Let's Talk Sexy: Essential Conversation Starters to Explore Your Lover's Secret Desires and Transform Your Sex Life

All **THREE** *Let's Talk About...* sexy question books in one massive volume for one low price. Save now!

Let's Talk About... Sexual Fantasies and Desires: Questions and Conversation Starters for Couples Exploring Their Sexual Interests

Let's Talk About... Non-Monogamy: Questions and Conversation Starters for Couples Exploring Open Relationships, Swinging, or Polyamory

Let's Talk About... Kinks and Fetishes: Questions and Conversation Starters for Couples Exploring Their Sexual Wild Side

Change your sex life forever through the power of sexy fun with your spouse, partner, or lover!

www.sexygamesforcouples.com

Sexy Vacations for Couples
https://geni.us/Passion

ABOUT THE AUTHOR

J.R. James is a best-selling author who has a passion for bringing couples closer together and recharging their sexual intimacy. Erotic discussion is a powerfully sexy thing, and his conversation starter books have helped many couples reach new and sexually exciting heights in their relationships!

Sexy conversation with your partner is a magical, bonding experience. Through these best-selling question books, couples can find an easy way to engage in open and honest sexual discussion with each other. The result is a relationship that is both erotically charged and sexually liberating.

jrjameslove@gmail.com
www.sexygamesforcouples.com

Made in the USA
Las Vegas, NV
22 November 2020